DATE			

for
Mary Ruth

OVER THE RIVER

AND THROUGH THE WOOD

by
Lydia Maria Child

pictures by
Brinton Turkle

COWARD-McCANN, INC.   NEW YORK

ver the river, and through the wood,
To grandfather's house we go;

The horse knows the way
To carry the sleigh,
Through the white and drifted snow.

ver the river, and through the wood,
To grandfather's house away!
We would not stop
For doll or top,
For 'tis Thanksgiving Day.

ver the river, and through the wood—
Oh, how the wind does blow!

It stings the toes,
And bites the nose,
As over the ground we go.

ver the river, and through the wood,
With a clear blue winter sky,
The dogs do bark,
And children hark,
As we go jingling by.

ver the river and through the wood,
To have a first-rate play.

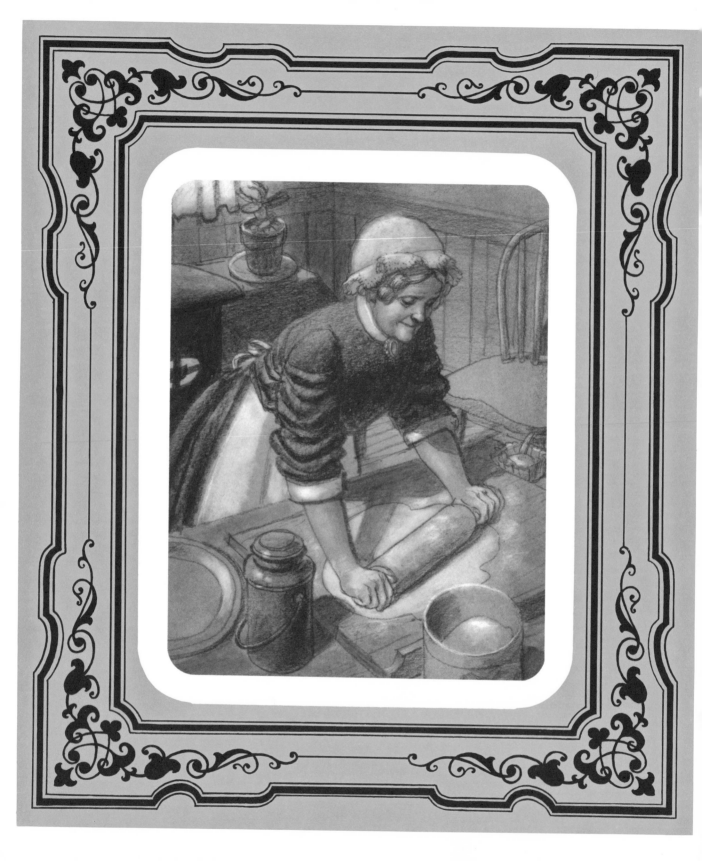

Hear the bells ring,
"Ting-a-ling-ding!"
Hurrah for Thanksgiving Day!

ver the river, and through the wood—
No matter for winds that blow;
Or if we get
The sleigh upset,
Into a bank of snow.

ver the river, and through the wood,
To see little John and Ann;

We will kiss them all,
And play snowball,
And stay as long as we can.

Over the river and through the wood
Trot fast my dapple-gray!
Spring over the ground
Like a hunting-hound!
For 'tis Thanksgiving Day.

Over the river and through the wood,
And straight through the barnyard gate.

We seem to go
Extremely slow—
It is so hard to wait!

ver the river, and through the wood—
Old Jowler hears our bells;
He shakes his pow,
With a loud bow-wow,
And thus the news he tells.

ver the river, and through the wood—
When grandmother sees us come,

She will say, "Oh, dear,
The children are here,
bring a pie for every one."

ver the river and through the wood—
Now grandmother's cap I spy!
Hurrah for the fun!
Is the pudding done?
Hurrah for the pumpkin-pie!

OVER THE RIVER

Allegretto   Traditional Song

O-ver the riv-er, and through the wood, To grand-fa-ther's house we go; _____ The
O-ver the riv-er, and through the wood—When grand-mo-ther sees us come, _____ She

horse knows the way to carry the sleigh through the white and drift-ed snow. _____
will say, "Oh, dear, the chil-dren are here, bring a pie for ever-y one." _____

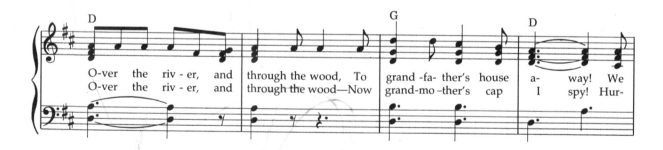

O-ver the riv-er, and through the wood, To grand-fa-ther's house a-way! We
O-ver the riv-er, and through the wood—Now grand-mo-ther's cap I spy! Hur-

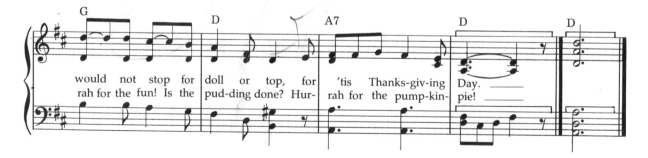

would not stop for doll or top, for 'tis Thanks-giv-ing Day.
rah for the fun! Is the pud-ding done? Hur-rah for the pump-kin-pie!